Whiskey in your coffee

100 SHORT STORIES TO REMIND YOU TO LIVE WITH GRIT,
GRACE AND GO FOR THE LIFE OF YOUR DREAMS

Nikki Glandon

ISBN 13: 9781670874573

Table of Contents

Intro 1
Brokin 3
Grace 4
Grit 5
Whiskey in Your Coffee 6
Howling Dogs 8
Blisters 9
Your Shadow 10
Special Blend 11
Singing out Loud 12
The Next Thing 13
Shelby Mustang 14
Love is Enough 15
Guitar 16
Road Trips 17
Plant Seeds 18
Looking.Other. Spaces. Too. (L.O.S.T) 19
Apple Pie 20
Celebrate 21
Beating Heart 22
Costume Box 23
Dance Party 24
More Music 25
The Table 26
Race Cars 27

Soften 28
Tennessee Football 29
8 Second Ride 31
ESPN 32
Help. 33
Bucked Off. 34
The Ringmaster 35
Curly Hair 36
Recipes. 37
Socks. 38
Fish Tank 39
The Stance 40
Rainmaker 41
Normal or Weird 42
Tattoos 43
Recharge. 44
Stages. 45
Warm Butter. 46
Old Journals 47
Pizza in Bed. 48
First Place 49
Stone. 50
Wild Child 51
Popcorn 52
Tennis Balls 53
Game Trails 54
Aspen Trees 55
Jacket. 56
The Zipper. 57
The Trailer 58
The Trailer Part 2. 59
Scars 60
Rip to Heal 61
Snakes. 62

Sharks 63

Superglue 64

First Aid Kit 65

Some Time 66

The Sweet Stuff 67

Puzzle Pieces 68

Relax and Breathe 69

Doing Dishes 71

Ocean Money 72

Serving Heart 73

Really Dream 75

Real love 76

3 Amazing Women 77

Escape Artist 78

Cowboys and Indians 79

Green Grass 80

Little Girl 81

Spirit Animal 82

Beachball 83

Fearless 84

Trust Yourself 85

Overtaking 86

Impact 87

Compliments 88

Hat Pin 89

Alone 90

Angel Babies 91

Soulfight 93

Happier 94

Stained Glass 95

Chicken Wings 96

Rockstar 97

Magic Wand 98

Goddess 99
Asking Too Much 100
Caged Tiger 101
All The Lights On 102
Dance Team 103
I Did Something Wrong 104
Keep Ehe Wolves Away 105
Pirates 106
Parking Tickets 107
Badass Sister 108

About the Author 109

Intro

I have had moments so low, that they led me to be hospitalized for suicide twice. I thought it would be easier if I just left. I felt like I was nothing but a burden to everyone around me. I couldn't call my mom or best friend crying anymore. I felt hopeless.

I had tried it all, therapy, medication, new job, new place to live, new relationship; but the emptiness I felt followed me everywhere like this lingering cloud over my head that was never going to go away. In my world, wanting to take my life was so far from selfish; and I thought everyone's lives would be better if I was gone.

That place is so dark. It's so scary. It's why I am talking about it. If it helps save one life by saying, "I've been there, I get it. You're not alone," it's worth writing this book. So many times we don't talk about this because of pride, the stigma; and we lose our loved ones. We suffer in ways we don't have to.

I can't say I never feel that way now, those moments when it feels like the black cloud is going to get me again, but I know that it won't and I am stronger because of my stories. The difference now is, I love myself. It took time, lots of patience and digging deep to do the work so that I can enjoy this one life that I have. It took just being me, Brokin and all.

You don't have to get to that point where you think the only way out is to end it. Sometimes it means taking one day at a time, sometimes 8 seconds at a time. Sometimes it might feel so low and lonely; but you're not alone. You're magnificent and so many people need you. You can get through it, no matter how low it feels. You are a miracle, be here. We need you. The world needs you.

This book is just one more way to allow us to talk about it, all of it, no matter what it is. Then, to talk about the tools, to let it go, to slow down your mind and breathe. To talk about loving yourself no matter what. I live with grit and grace everyday. More days now are just peaceful; but learning to love myself, that was the hardest thing I ever did.

I hope this book does just that, reminds you to love yourself, to live wild and to go for your dreams. I hope this book encourages conversation for us to share our stories, to lift each other up, and to find more laughter.

Brokin

I love boots, especially really comfy, "Brokin" cowboy boots.
The good ones, that have been
through the mud, but only to have come out on the other side,
brokin and all.
They are so easy to slide onto my feet. I can wear them all day.
They are cute (this matters), and I am nothing but comfortable.

We're all a "little brokin." We've been through the grit, but
we came out on the other side a comfier in our own skin,
like that old pair of jeans or boots that are perfectly worn in.

"Brokin," is a way of living with grit and grace, because you live
with all the stories that made you who you are today.

So many of the moments I share in this book are to
remind you that you've got this; that you are amazing the
way you are and to allow yourself grace on the days you need
it, grit on the others.

To love who you are, share
your story, good and bad, to live free, with light and laughter
and most importantly love and rock all of who you are brokin
and all. What's better than you being you, all of you just like a
great pair of Brokin Boots?

Grace

Grace is peace in you. It's the place where you can feel. You breathe. Grace is laughter in the hard times. It creates warmth in your heart and calmness in pain. Grace is a sweet hug and the phrase, "I'm not okay." Grace is within all of us. It's the moments of being okay with not being okay. Of moving through, so you can be magnificent. Grace is crying on the bathroom floor and calling a friend to say, "I need you."

Grace is the moment you realize you're perfect as you are and there is strength in softness. It's when you realize everything is okay, always has been and always will be. It's the time when you can laugh at your mistakes, your moments of so-called weakness. Grace is the reminder you are not weak but strong and free. Grace is the moment you allow yourself to be. To let go. Know you always have grace. It always lives in you.

Grit

G rit is when you find something you love and you keep going for it, nothing can stop you.

Grit comes from knowing who you are, what you stand for and what you want to bring to this world. Without grit, without sticking in there and letting go of what everyone else thinks, you'll just stay on the sidelines.

When I talk about grit, I don't mean forcing things to happen or back-breaking work. The grit comes from loving all of you and knowing what you desire. When you get clear on those things, that grit that lives inside you keep you going despite your obstacles. Grit is courage in the storm, passion, vulnerability, and perseverance for your one life. Grit gives you the strength of a warrior to move through the obstacles, all the while giving yourself the grace of a goddess.

Whiskey in Your Coffee

'm sitting here trying to write this book. Fighting back the tears, thinking, "What the hell am I doing? No one is going to read this. Who do you think you are?" It feels like a "Whiskey in my Coffee" kind of day. See, the name "Whiskey in Your Coffee" is more of a metaphor, though trust me, some days I do add some to my coffee.

The title of this book all started with a phrase my best friend and I would say, "Feels like a whiskey in our coffee kind of day." It was a joke. Well, most of the time; but it was our way of saying, "Man, today feels heavy already." You know what I mean--those days where it starts feeling off; where you want to crawl back into bed; where a little whiskey in your coffee is the only way you will get through it. The good news is, it's perfectly okay to have those days. It's a metaphor for those days when my mind swirls and says things like, "What the hell am I doing?" "Who am I?" or "How am I gonna get through this?" Whiskey in my coffee is the only way, throw in the towel.

This seems to happen when I'm on the right path. It's never when I am running away or hiding that my brain starts to go into overdrive. It's always when I'm going for it and taking leaps of faith and trusting, when fear sneaks into my head. This is where grit comes in. This is when I look upon my own fear and tell it to "Take a seat. I've got work to do." I often have to tell "fear" to get out or "Not today Satan."

Do you ever have times like that? When your brain is swirling with everything negative? Those days feel so terribly awful, but you will survive days like that. Survive the moments when you're being attacked. It begins with breathing slowly.

Those days happen, but that is not meant to be your life. You are meant to thrive, so you can live your wildest dreams. Your life is meant to be filled with love, laughter, and joy. Your life is a collection of stories that make you who you are, brokin and all.

It takes grit and a lot of trust. I promise that all you have to do is just shift your focus to stop the swirling. You can do it. Go write your book. Sing your song. Do whatever it is you desire. Take the leap. Show this world how magical you are. What leap can you take today that will start you on the path to your dreams?

Howling Dogs

There are these dogs that live near me. They don't bark. They howl. When they do, it starts the game with my neighbor's dog that chirps. It's like, "Let's see who can get the loudest for the longest." Let me tell you, it is not fun when they do it.

This is the kind of thing we often do in life. Trying to speak the loudest to prove our point, ends up being exhausting for all parties involved. What if we tried another way? Because there always is another way.

We have a tendency to want to win at all costs, to howl louder, and get all the neighbors involved. When really if we just laid down and stopped howling, there's a good chance all of the external chatter would quiet also. There is no need to exhaust ourselves chirping when the best thing to do is to let it be and stop stirring the pot.

We can only control ourselves, and when we learn that, our world will become so much more peaceful. All of the howling dogs around us will seem to back down as well.

Where in your life is an area that you can stop howling?

Blisters

B listers hurt, are no fun, and in my case, they come from trying to prove a point. On this particular occasion, I was building a fence, which I did build, but at the sacrifice of my hands, and, of course, I refused to ask for help. That's often the case for me, stubborn. The blisters hurt, and I would have rather been cooking dinner.

I realized there is always a lesson in something if we take the time to listen. The lesson for me was slow down before I make choices because I didn't end up even needing the fence. I rushed in too fast and went through pain I didn't need to experience. Why do we do that to ourselves? Try to prove we can do something when instead it hurts us? It seems pretty stupid if you ask me. All we have to do is ask for help.

As I was building that fence, I remembered that God is by my side no matter what. I can tell you; I may not have seen anyone else by my side building that fence, but I wasn't alone. God helped me build that fence because I couldn't really do it on my own. He gave me strength when I had none and when the blisters were burning. I realized you are never alone, even in those moments, when you feel completely alone, you are not. You're not alone because someone else out there is feeling what you're feeling and because God is with you. You are not alone, no need for blisters. Just Ask.

Your Shadow

I have this one horse, Waylon. He's big, beautiful, strong, loving, kind, and powerful, yet terrified of his own shadow. It's like he wouldn't know what to do if he realized how strong he is. What would it be like if you released your potential, if you showed the world what you're made of instead of being afraid of it? Can you imagine how that would feel?

It tends to be our full power that we are afraid of, showing up with all you were made to do and be. You just have to learn how to release your own power and not be afraid.

Begin to visualize the life you want, and how you show up in that life. Who are you being? To be the big creation machine you are, you will need to step outside of your comfort zone and show up. It's your time.

Time to play big.

Time to unleash your full potential and to stop being afraid of your own shadow.

Are you afraid of your own shadow, of unleashing all your power to your full potential? Time to show the world what you are made of.

Special Blend

We are all unique, special, crazy, and quirky; our own special blend. Somewhere along the way, it seems we were told we had to be perfect, ordinary, average; but here's the best news.

You are perfect exactly how you are. You are your own unique blend of sweet, spicy, strong, soft, classic and rustic. You are your very own blend. So go ahead and BE you, all of you, no matter what.

Your blend changes a little each day, so embrace who you are today. As you grow and evolve, little pieces of you will shift. Over time, you will know exactly who you are and what your blend is. You can be a little of this and a little of that. You can like new things. Let go of things you used to like. Shake it up. See what feels right.

At the end of the day, the goal is for it to feel right to you. So be a little spicy, a little sweet, and a hot. No matter what, be your own special blend.

What makes you, you?

What would you call your special blend if you named it?

Singing out Loud

I sang in front of someone today for the first time since 6th grade. See, I didn't make 6th-grade chorus and as my good buddy said, "Nikki, did we even have to try out for 6th-grade chorus?" Meaning "everyone" made 6th-grade chorus but me! You see, we had to have a musical elective. When I didn't make chorus, band it was; and I was forced to play saxophone in the band. Band at that time was for the nerdy kids. All the cool kids made chorus—at least that was the story I told myself.

Well, I held onto the story that I couldn't sing and feared singing. That shut my voice down for years. Now, 20 years later, I finally let that fear go.

I know that my voice is going to need some work, but I started. That's all that matters, and it is about so much more than singing.

It is about me using my authentic voice, as well. This story taught me that even if my voice shakes, share my truth. Honor who I am and don't hold back. Now, I get to keep going and learn to sing, to really belt it out. I had to start. I had to let go of a stupid fear from 20 years ago.

It's your turn. Let the world know your story. What fear is in the way, what's stopping you from having fun, from growing and really sharing your voice?

I can tell you, let that story go, it's so much better on the other side. Go sing out loud.

The Next Thing

I am really good at finding a way out. A way to avoid and run, like suddenly, I need to go to the grocery store, fold laundry. Hell, I'll even clean the bathroom, just to avoid working on what I really want in life because I'm afraid of what if it's not good enough, what will people think?

When I think about that, it is so dumb. It just makes it so my dreams take longer to come to life. I stop myself cold because I'm afraid. What am I really afraid of, someone not liking me, or what I do? Of being successful? It's so *dumb* to be afraid. I'm going to do The Next Thing.

When we let go of worry, of judgment, all doors will open. You will begin to show the world your gifts and live freely. It's like you finally begin to live.

So today, just do the next thing that sets you on your path to the life *you* want. Not a life for anyone else. When you start from the place of just doing the next thing, you shift your energy. You open up to possibility. It's like all of a sudden you shout, "Yes! I am able, and I am going to just do the next thing." Micro-movements add up and quickly. Today, just do the next thing. Keep it simple and remember you don't climb Everest in one step.

Shelby Mustang

There are days when I feel like I am a sexy '67 Shelby Mustang. You couldn't catch me if you tried. Days like that are fun and exhilarating, and I am unstoppable. I've had days where I'm the car that is stuck in the garage, suspended wheels spinning and I am not going anywhere. On days like that, I need someone to come pick me up and take me for a cruise on a backcountry road and remind me, I've got this.

I'm very grateful to have friends in my life that I can call up on the phone and hear, "You're not in this alone." Trust me, I want to be that Shelby every day; but then I would miss out on that slow drive with my friend who maybe needed me that day too.

This is a great check-in for yourself. Life changes from day to day, and so do you. Work from there, meet yourself where you're at. So many times we don't meet ourselves where we are in the moment. Instead, we try to push through and not give ourselves grace.

So, no matter what car you are today or tomorrow, meet yourself there. Give yourself grace and enjoy the drive.

Ask yourself, what kind of car am I today?

Love is Enough

Who started the phrase "Love isn't enough?" If love isn't enough, what is? The most profound definition of love I've ever found is, "Love is patient. Love is kind. It does not envy. It does not boast. It is not proud. It is not rude. It is not self-seeking. It is not easily angered. It keeps no record of wrongs. Love does not delight in evil but rejoices with the truth. It always protects, always trusts, always hopes, always perseveres." I Corinthians 13:4-7

Love is everything.

So, let's remove the stigma around "Love is enough" and start living by the definition of love. Then try to say it's not enough. Love will solve everything.

Try it out today--be patient, kind, forgiving, gentle because when you start living by the definition of love, you will see it is enough. Try starting with yourself. Love is not one thing. It is all-encompassing.

How can you show love in a new way today?

Guitar

Years ago, I said I wanted to learn how to play guitar. So, I got a guitar for my birthday. Well, as life goes, things changed and the guitar started collecting dust.

Two years later, I needed something to take my mind off the divorce I was in the middle of, something to help heal me. I picked up the guitar, dusted it off, signed up for lessons, and went for it. I am pretty sure I played the same two chords over and over for months, but it allowed my brain to stop being in overdrive. It also made me put the glass of wine down since I couldn't play with one hand. I knew I needed a creative outlet, something for my brain to learn and my heart to heal.

Now, I can play a few songs, and I gain more traction every day. More importantly, I did something for me--something I said I wanted. I went for it. I had to let go of the fear of judgment about how bad it sounded because it wasn't for anyone else. It was for me and still is.

When was the last time you did something for you? Something you have put on the shelf, on hold, it's collecting dust. Go get it off the proverbial shelf. Wipe it off and start for you. Because if you don't, who will?

Road Trips

Do you enjoy the drive or only getting to the destination? There are so many amazing experiences that happen on road trips. Why do we tend to lose sight of them? Some of the best conversations, family games, memories, new jamming songs, and beautiful views all happen on the journey to the destination. Even the dreaded question, "Are we there yet?" is a blessing. See, the trip doesn't start when you get there. It starts with the planning.

Why do we let the journey, sometimes the best part, disappear so quickly? I have never been good at letting it be a journey. I have always wanted to get to the goal or destination quickly, sometimes missing a cool song or view along the way.

I'm learning to slow down, to enjoy the drive and everything that comes with it. I'm learning that the twists and turns are what it is about because those get you to the top of the mountain. Don't make a u-turn because the drive got a little curvy. Enjoy the rolling hills, the mountain passes, and most importantly, enjoy the journey. It's the only one you have.

Plant Seeds

Have you ever stopped and looked at a garden and thought about how it grows?

I'm no green-thumb, unlike my Dad. He can grow anything. I kill aloe plants. Do you know how hard that is to do? Lately, I started learning more about gardening. Learning that it's the simple things that make a difference like oh ya I need to water the garden.

For instance, all gardens start as seeds and *grow* into a beautiful garden when planted in good soil and are tended to with care.

I'm learning that how you tend the garden is what matters. Like, if I forget to water the seeds, there is no growth.

I've also learned that nature does not mess up. It doesn't rush or worry about how to make the garden grow. It just grows at its own rate.

Just like the garden, our dreams and goals are seeds. They need to be planted in good, rich soil. The soil of who you are, and how you are showing up in the world--is your soil positive or negative?

Are you pushing and pushing, worrying and worrying? If so, try acting like nature, and just grow with ease and peace. Remember, just like seeds in a garden, it takes time to grow, so keep tending and watering your dreams. Let God do the rest. Your dreams will take off.

Nikki Glandon

Looking.Other. Spaces. Too. (L.O.S.T)

Have you ever felt lost? Stuck? What's next? Where do I go from here?

What if lost was no longer scary but simply meant:

Looking.Other. Spaces. Too.

Sometimes feeling lost is just a way that the universe raises its hand and says, "Hey you! Hey you! Look over here!"

Feeling lost is hard, but being lost is a way to lead you to a new path, a chance to navigate the waters and choose your new journey.

I think being "lost" has more positivity than we give it credit. It is a way to push yourself, to help you figure out the next path, to look at other spaces too. You can start to explore a new path, a new outlook, and have fun on the adventure.

Today, I encourage you to get L.O.S.T. Try something new, maybe somewhat scary.

Open up to the possibilities and always have fun.

'Cause that's the point right?

Apple Pie

Who doesn't love a homemade apple pie? They are sweet and savory. The delicious ones are filled with butter and love. It's not the recipe that makes the pie delicious; it's the intention behind it. When we do things with love, it changes everything.

Think about homemade pie--like the one your grandma, mom or someone who took their precious time to make the best pie for you. Yes, just for you. Imagine walking into their house where you can smell the pie. Their kitchen and hands are covered in flour, butter, sugar and cinnamon. Most importantly, you feel the love going into that pie.

You know that the very intention behind that mess is love for you and your taste buds. How does that feel, that the mess was for you? You see, when you choose to do something with love; it makes everything taste better, just like a warm apple pie.

Think about the last time you did something with the intention of love. How did it feel? Today, remember that feeling and try to approach even the small things from the purpose of love. Get out there, cover your hands in flour, get your kitchen messy and show up with love. It's the little things, like a homemade apple pie, that will always make someone feel warm and loved.

Nikki Glandon

Celebrate

We celebrate birthdays, anniversaries, and our significant accomplishments. Why do we forget to celebrate the little things? Like when you went to the gym or signed up for a new educational course, you sent one email from your new account, or celebrate, that today, you woke up.

What is one goal you could take "The Leap" toward? Go to your first yoga class? Start on the project you keep putting off, or maybe remove one unhealthy item from your diet? Do it. Then celebrate, because the first step is the hardest. You will see how each step you take forward adds up to many steps and those steps add up faster than you think.

Think about it this way. You have decided to run a marathon. Your first step is not to run the 26 miles. The first step is going to look at some new running shoes. Then put them on your feet. Then take ONE step. Then after some time, mile by mile you make it to your first marathon. So go ahead and be stoked about your running shoes. Be excited that you have a new goal, and then celebrate whatever it may be. What is something you can celebrate right now?

Beating Heart

In the heart, each cell is beating continuously. If we were to dissect the heart, each cell would continue to beat by itself. When we put the cells with other heart cells, the cells shift their rhythm so they beat together. Isn't that incredible? By taking time to tune into your own heartbeat, you connect not only with yourself, but the rhythm of the world around you as well.

One way to connect to your heart better is to simply breathe. Breath is the key to life, without breath, there is no life. We take about 20,000 breaths a day, which is around 5,000 gallons of air. Breathing is vital for life and for the opening of the heart. Breath is regulated by the circulatory system each breath nourishes and rejuvenates the circulatory system. See the connection?

Start with noticing the breath. What does it feel like to pause and fill up with a full breath? Since the body speaks to the mind, what is the area around your heart saying, your chest, your lungs? Does it feel constricted? Maybe it's time to receive a deep breath. You see, an open heart isn't weak or soft; it's actually the opposite. It is full of light, love, and strength.

Slow down and take a breath. Send it to the heart and mind. Nurture yourself with the gift of breath that is given to us in such abundant supply.

Costume Box

J ust because it's not Halloween doesn't mean you have to put away your costume box. Halloween is a beautiful way to bring out your childlike side. To bust out the costume box, get creative and have fun! Why do we feel like we need a holiday to bring out our inner child?

What if you started looking at life like a child does? With curiosity, playfulness, and wonderment. Life is magical, and everywhere you look, there is a wonderment.

For some reason, as adults, we feel as if we have to be "grown-up" and not have curiosity anymore. Children often remind us to laugh, have fun and look at the joys around us. What if you had fun no matter what you were doing? What if you found your inner child? At the end of the day, isn't that what life is about--laughing, smiling, playing?

So remember that fun doesn't have to be just one day of the year. We can always get out our costume box, and you can still be whoever or whatever you want to be. Just go for it and have fun along the way.

Dance Party

When was the last time you felt free and not like you're just living a daily checklist? When was the last time you danced it out? What would happen if you let go of the grip and stopped trying so hard for everything to be perfect? What if you allowed your mind and body to move freely without judgment, logic, or order?

It's time to grab some headphones and to let the right side of your brain lead, even if for just a minute. The right side is non-verbal, creative and feeling. When was the last time you just felt?

We need to make sure we take time to lead with the right side, to tap into the energy and creativity we have and not always focus on the "supposed to's and shoulds." We need to slow down enough to listen to what our body is feeling so that we can be open to creative solutions. Doing this can not only create more happiness but also change your view and activate your intuition.

So let go of the checklist, the practical, the logical, and have a DANCE PARTY instead. Let your freedom lead your love and intuition, honestly just let go. Dance it out. No one is watching and if they are…show them your moves.

More Music

W e are all born with music inside us, and it's letting your song play that can be a challenge.

Have you ever tried walking to someone else's beat? How did it feel? Were you always out of rhythm?

The most important thing we can do in life, is be ourselves, which means walking to your own beat, your rhythm. When you start to love the music inside of you, it may seem as if life is a little more natural, like you are no longer swimming upstream.

First, start with identifying your beat, who are you? What brings you joy and happiness? Getting clear on who you are, opens doors of possibility you never thought existed.

I am a little of everything, rock, country, hip-hop, oldies, it depends on the day or maybe even the moment. That's how wonderful life is. Moment to moment things can change so knowing what your beat is, your music, it will help you move through the changes.

No matter what it is, rock it. Always rock who you are because the world needs you. Even the days when you have the same sappy love song on repeat, rock it because the world needs your music.

The Table

What do you bring to the table, no matter what it looks like or who is there?

It might be a table just for you, and that is perfect. Or is it a meal with friends or family? No matter the labels or people at the table, what do you bring?

How do you show up at the table of life? The table is a metaphor, just one more way to look at life.

Are you the person that shows up with open arms filled with love to give? Perfect.

Do you need love and hugs? Perfect.

Are you showing up with pies and turkeys for days because you have the time, and you made them? Perfect.

Are you showing up with the most exquisite bottle of wine? Perfect.

No matter where you are or what you can bring to the table, know that it is precisely where you are supposed to be. Sometimes, we have more to give, more time, love, money. Sometimes we have less. That is called life balance. It's why showing up exactly how you are is the perfect thing you can do. So show up. Be real. Be you. Always know you have a place at the table.

Race Cars

There was a recent conversation with a 2-year old that went something like this…" Connor, what do you want for your birthday?" "New race cars" was the response. Connor, what else do you want for your birthday?" This time, with a puzzled face, the response was "New race cars" knowing that all he wanted was new race cars. There was nothing else.

It was so simple, so pure and so joyful. Sometimes the simplicity in life can get lost. The to-do list gets longer, and you feel drained instead of vibrant. What would happen if you let it be simple and as easy, finding enjoyment along the way?

Stop to look around, to enjoy the smells, the music, the laughter. Let it be enjoyable instead of driving your car around like it is a new race car from place to place. Slow down. Be in the moment. Be where you are at. Be present and still.

You'll be surprised at what can occur in simplicity and stillness. Your minivan is not a race car, even if you think it is. What joy can you find in simplicity?

Soften

In certain types of equine massage, the work is done with macro-movements and by softening or backing off. Horses can't verbally tell us it is too much, so we have to pay attention to the body language.

I find this is often the case with challenges of life. This is where a little grace in your life will help you feel the tension in that area. When you start to bring this softening technique into your life, you will notice the tension will begin to release.

Allow yourself a moment to step back and notice what's going on, observing and releasing. So many times, we find ourselves trying to power through something, coming out exhausted and still not accomplishing our goal.

Try a new way today. Soften. Notice how the tension will begin to work itself out. Our bodies and lives have a way of working things out when we allow them space. Stop bracing against life, take a step back, and create room for the tension to release.

Right now, check-in with your jaw. Are you clenching it without even realizing? All you have to do is soften.

Tennessee Football

I am born and raised a Tennessee girl. There is an old phrase, "You can take the girl out of the country, but you can't take the country out of the girl." So with that being said. I bleed orange! Go Vols! Born and bred this way because of the memories with my family, my dad.

The thing is, Tennessee football is currently awful and has been for years. Shhh, don't tell them I said this. But it does not remove my love for the memories of the times I spent at the games. What it does, is teach me about attachment and what I put my energy into.

Is there something in your life that you put so much into that no matter what happens, it will affect you? When we learn to let go of attachment and circumstances, we can gain our true power.

It's the attachment to the thing, like the score of the game, not the game itself. Letting go of attachment to the outcome will allow you to enjoy so much more. What if you allowed yourself to let go of attachment to a certain outcome, and be open to God's path? When we let go, it creates freedom, openness, faith. When we cling, it drains us. It takes time away from our precious lives. Allow the good from the situation to remain and let go of the rest.

Just like with the Vols, I love the memories of my friends and family, but I can't keep holding my breath waiting on them to win. I had to let go of them winning and just enjoy the game itself.

8 Second Ride

Life is a lot like an 8-second ride. Anything can happen. From the second a cowboy is in the shoot to the end of the 8 seconds, that bull can go right, left, up, down, and you never know which combo he is going to give on that given day.

Like life, we don't know what is ahead, what combo we are going to get on that given day; but I think there is magic in knowing anything can happen in 8 seconds, and the fun is enjoying the ride. Let's call it an 8-second shift. In 8 seconds you can change your thinking, you can quiet your mind, you can shift in 8 seconds.

When you are feeling hopeless, defeated like nothing is going to change, remember anything can happen in 8 seconds. Then you can go for 8 seconds at a time. That will add up and before you know you've hung on for the full ride.

You've been doing the work; the process is happening. Your journey is leading you to that 8-second change where all the practice has paid off. Don't give up. Remember, anything can happen in 8 seconds. Have fun on your ride.

ESPN

In high school, my dance team got second in the nation at a National Competition, and we were on ESPN! Yep, I still talk about it today. (Mainly to annoy my brother) It was fun and surely the claim to my 15 minutes of fame, but now it's just a family joke.

Well, I found out my 10-year-old niece was possibly going to be on ESPN for volleyball; and I said, "No, that means she wins because she was on ESPN younger than I was!" Of course, my brother and I were cracking up about this. The funny thing was, it ended up being my 3- year-old nephew who made the big screen that day for ESPN. All I did was laugh. Then it made me think about how many times I have let someone else steal my thunder, and why I would think someone could do that, take away from who I am, what I have and what I have accomplished.

This happens all the time to so many of us. We think someone is going to steal our thunder; take away our moment of fame. The thing is, no one can take our thunder, not even your 10-year-old niece or 3-year old nephew. It's yours and always will be.

How can you let go of thinking someone is going to do something better, bigger, faster, sooner than you, and rock your own thunder?

Help

I've started to ask for help, and let me tell you it is a game-changer. It hit me recently when I walked to my neighbor's to ask for milk. It felt like the good 'ole days where we helped each other out, when we knew our neighbors.

Sometimes it's the smallest things that wake us up, like asking for milk. It made me realize I don't have to do it on my own.

Why are we so afraid to ask for help, when most of us would gladly give help? What's the point of not asking? What do we win besides frustration, stress, and headache?

We are here to connect with each other, support, and help each other. By not asking or allowing help, we block the flow. We say, "I can do it all on my own."

Be the person that asks for help or the person that gives it because we need the flow. We need each other. Stop trying to play the game of life on your own and ask for help when you need it. Is there an area of life you need help, how much easier would it be to just ask for it?

Bucked Off

We all know the phrase, "Get back in the saddle." Well, if you have ever been bucked off a horse, you know it hurts. I got bucked off recently, and thank God, I got up and walked away just fine. The next day my body hurt, but we went riding, and I never even thought about not getting back in the saddle.

That's the point here. When you find something you're passionate about, getting back in the saddle is not hard. I think so many times we are trying to get back in the saddle, and it's not being afraid that stops us, but lack of passion.

It's important to really pay attention to the difference. Fear will step in and convince you to stay safe, to just go sit down and give up. Passion will trump fear every time. Passion will tell fear to take a seat, to be quiet, you've got work to do.

So, if you're not climbing back in the saddle, is it fear or lack of passion? When it's right, when you love it, you might get bucked off over and over; but you will overcome your fears and climb in the saddle every time.

Where in your life do you feel unstoppable no matter how many times you get "bucked off?"

The Ringmaster

W e tend to forget that we are the Ringmaster of our own lives and so often, just sit down to watch the show. If you have ever been to a circus or seen someone work with horses in the round pen, you can see that the Ringmaster is just that, the master.

In the round pen, sometimes we work with horses at liberty. Liberty training is designed to bring a horse a sense of freedom and safety without using any tack, including halters or ropes. When the horse and ringmaster are connected, the horse will continue to move without any physical command from the ringmaster.

The truth is, that is the same in life. When you are in flow and know you are the creator of your life, life will continue to move for you with grace and ease. But to accomplish being the ringmaster, you have to know that you are a writer, storyteller, and creator of your life. When you realize this all of a sudden, the doors fly open. You stop playing victim to your "circumstances" and realize you are your own ringmaster.

Are you the ringmaster of your life, or are you in the bleachers watching the show?

Curly Hair

When I was around 10, I got a perm that I really, really wanted. Then as soon as I saw it, I HATED IT! I said with tears in my eyes, "I look like a lion." The hairdresser told my mom and me it wouldn't last because I was young and my hair wouldn't hold the perm. Well, I have had curly hair since then--how's that for a perm that wouldn't last?

Now I love it! I rock it and embrace it. That was not always the case. I wanted straight hair. I wanted what I didn't have, instead of loving what I had.

How many times have you felt that way? If only I was skinnier, taller, smarter, blah, blah, blah. It's time we love ourselves, *all* of ourselves. Every little thing from your laugh lines, to your curly hair, your laugh, your thoughts, that little extra on your waist because your pie is so good, that time you had too much wine and called your ex. Love you and all of you. Let's stop putting each other down and realize we need each other. Start by loving yourself. Then you can't help but spread all that love to other people. So, whatever it is you "don't like about yourself" stop, because I guarantee someone else thinks it's beautiful and wonderful and perfect just as it is. Just like curly hair.

Recipes

I love to cook, and people will ask me for the recipe, which I never have. See, I am not a recipe kinda person. I'm more like, "Let's have some fun in the kitchen and see how it works" kind of gal.

While using no recipe really works in some aspects of life, in other areas, not so much. This allows freedom in my life but not necessarily consistency. As I get older, I am realizing how important both sides of that are--freedom and consistency. If I want my business to grow, my relationships to thrive and to be able to have freedom, I also need to get organized and have more of a plan that allows me to shift as needed.

I'm coming to realize that having the plan gives me room to be creative and breathe. It's the structure of the plan that helps me move forward so my vision can come to life. Just like a recipe, we can add in a little of this and that, or we can leave out what we don't like.

But the recipe? The structure? Well, it gives us room to be free because first it gives an outline, some structure, some clarity. Where in your life do you need more structure so you can have more freedom?

Socks

Ok, this is life's biggest mystery! Where do all of the socks go? You know what I mean. I put 2 perfectly good socks into the laundry and only one comes out. Does the dryer really eat them? I spent a good amount of my afternoon on a recent Sunday matching socks, wondering "Where do they all go and is this what being an adult is about? Why did I want to grow up so quickly, just to match socks?"

We see it all the time in kids. All they want to do is grow up, leave the house, have freedom. Do they not know with all that comes matching socks and wondering where did they all go?

We want to grow up so badly that we forget that life is a story, not just a goal line. As adults, we are always looking for the next thing, the end goal, something better all the while forgetting to be in the moment, to be present.

What would happen to you, if you started to live for today instead of longing for something else? If we don't start to slow down, to enjoy the moment, we will miss it all--the laughter, the tears, the lessons, the opportunity for change. We will miss what our friend is saying to us, or how good the food is. We will miss the smell of rain, the beauty of new snow all because we keep longing for the next thing, something else, something better and end up just matching socks.

Fish Tank

—

Divorce is not fun, and I could say mine was fairly easy; but I still felt like I had this big failure bubble over my head with the divorce label. I felt stuck like I was stuck in a fish tank just swimming and swimming wondering when I was going to be free from the confinement of this label. It felt like people looked at me wondering, "why he left or what's wrong with her?" Then, one day I realized I wasn't stuck in the tank. I was free. I was swimming and it all came on a girl's night out.

You see, my ex-husband lived down the road from me and every day I sat at the 4-way stop right in front of his house. Well, I sat there with my dear friend one night, where you could see right into his house and his TV. She looked at me and said, "I hate that fish screensaver, It's always on his TV." I burst out laughing and realizing, how funny it was that she hated it so much and most importantly I knew right then that then I was free, I wasn't stuck, I didn't have divorce or failure bubbles over my head. I wasn't stuck in the fish tank, but that I was me again, swimming free.

How can you remove and labels you have given yourself so you can feel free again?

The Stance

Do you know if you stand like Superwoman for 2 minutes it literally changes the hormones in your body? I think from now on we should all stand like Superwoman once a day for 2 minutes. Think of what that would do. Because the thing is, you are, you are Superwoman. Say that again.

You are capable of anything you want.

I think we put too much energy into what we don't do, don't have the mistakes we made, or the people we allow to take our power. Superwoman doesn't do that, she stands in her own power and does not question who she is.

Think about everything you do, feel, say, love, think. Everything about you is super. So feel it. Let it move through your soul, your being, all of you. Embrace that you are Superwoman and lift your chin higher. Stop thinking you're not. Stop letting other people convince you to believe less than that. What would happen if today you realized that being brave, vulnerable, kind, loving, courageous, heartfelt, and open made you Superwoman?

Rainmaker

There is this diagram called the drama triangle, it consists of the victim, the villain and the hero. Well, we have all been there before choosing to play one of those roles. When we remember we are the creator of our story, we step out of the triangle, the drama and become the rainmaker.

You get to choose to be the person that helps calm the storm instead of stepping in to create a bigger storm.

Do you find yourself constantly in one of those roles? Being the "Oh poor me victim?" Or are you the villain blaming others, not taking responsibility for your own actions? Or do you always show up trying to save the day, trying to prove your worth as a hero, but keeping the victim down?

So many times it's easy to find yourself in the drama triangle and becoming addicted to one of the roles, to the drama. These moments in our lives we let the story control us instead of realizing we are choosing the story. How much peace would you have if you become the rainmaker, the person that brings peace and calms the storm? The person that does not become part of the drama triangle but steps out of and breaks the cycle?

Normal or Weird

had a 10-year-old ask me if I would rather be normal or weird and without hesitation, I said "Weird." When I think about that question. what is normal and what is weird? Who came up with those parameters? Who put us in those categories? Where truly, the best category to be in, is simply you. You are so much bigger than any category or feeling like you have to be normal or weird, or finding some box to put yourself in. Why even choose one?

I think next time someone asks me that question I am going to say, "Me." I would rather be me, which is a little of everything because I no longer want to live in a category, but I want to live fully, freely following my own path my heart. To someone that might be "normal," to someone else it might be "weird," but either way, it doesn't matter because I know who I am and I choose the category.

What category do you put yourself in, how does it feel?

Tattoos

M y first tattoo was not small. It was the definition of "Go big or go home." I got half of my upper arm done. Years later, I now have one fully tattooed arm and a few other small ones. They are mine. There are not other tattoos that are the same, yet I still compare myself and my tattoos.

I have this beautiful girlfriend who has a couple tattoos. She's one of my dearest friends. People tell us we look like sisters. Time and time again I compare myself to her. I think, "Man, those tattoos look great on her. She's beautiful. She's successful." Why do we do this--the comparison game? Well, the truth is we choose to, we let our brains go into overdrive of comparing instead of practicing self-love.

You are a unique badass exactly as you are. Love you. Own you. Rock you. Stop comparing yourself to other women. It keeps you stuck. It lowers your energy. It robs you of your magic. Today, give a woman a compliment. Change her day. It will change your life.

Recharge

How many times have you said, "I don't have time." I hate to burst your bubble, but you are choosing to not have the time. We have the time, we just choose to sacrifice the desires of our souls to things we are "supposed to" or "should do."

It's important to take the time to sit in the hammock, read a book, take a bath, put the headphones on for one song. If we don't chill out, we run out. We drain ourselves. Our bodies get sick.

I challenge you to take time to breathe. Start with a 5-10 minute walk or one minute to sit in the sunshine to help you recharge. Choose something daily to fill your soul. Then you won't run your tank all the way down. It's time to let go of the belief that you don't have the time and listen to your heart, that voice that says, "Relax. Enjoy the time for you."

How can you give yourself some hammock time today?

Stages

W e have different names for stages in our lives, like infant, toddler, teenager, adult, etc. Yet, we tend to forget that we have other stages too. Sometimes those stages are years, months, days, hours; and they change all the time.

When taking life down into smaller chunks, we can navigate the waters better. We can allow the change process to happen, to move through the stages. I have been in stages of life where I have been tired, drained, and I need a break. Other times I'm ready to go, fired up. Stages where I needed to be alone and others where I am the life of the party. Sometimes it's a day; sometimes it's years.

Remembering the keyword here is stages, like building blocks no matter where you are, that stage is teaching you and changing you so you can show up and fulfill your destiny. The important part is enjoying where you are, not looking forward or back but being there now.

What stage of life are you at right now? How can you find a blessing in it no matter what?

Warm Butter

I have a few nicknames, but one of them is "Butterballs," and it's because I love to cook with butter and I have a soft heart. It's open, gooey, and full of love (and butter).

Having a soft heart has definitely caused me much pain at times, but in the end, way more love. I have thought I was weak because I have a soft heart, but now I know it is one of my gifts, my superpowers. It reminds me of warm butter in a pan, how it melts perfectly and just takes up the whole pan.

I think that's what a soft heart does, it allows you to spread your love, to wrap someone in your arms and feel them melt into you. If your heart is cold and not able to melt, it stays in one place, cold and rigid, hard to cut through. Think about how much better a warm, soft heart is. Just like hot butter, you can spread that love all over the place.

How can you soften today, warm your heart up to the people around you?

Nikki Glandon

Old Journals

Have you ever read your old journals and wondered who wrote this shit? I mean really like, was I crazy, or lost or who was I? Then, I knew I was perfect; that's where I was at in life at that moment. That is what I felt, and it was a layer of me, an aspect of me. I wrote it because it was important to me, and I needed to get it out. That is what matters.

If we don't get it out of our thoughts and feelings, if we keep them all locked up, we tend to stay in the same pattern instead of growing and peeling back the layers.

Those journals. Those old ways of being are important. They are all part of your story, and you wouldn't be where you are today without your story. I laugh and enjoy my old journals. They are part of me, my story and who I am today. I still may not want anyone else to read them, but if they do, I will rock it and proudly take credit because that is part of my story, my journey, and without that, I would not be where I am at today!

Is there a part of your story you would like to get rid of, how can you embrace that side of you, shine a light on it?

Pizza in Bed

I made dinner one night. Ate it. Then I made a frozen pizza, drank red wine, and then I watched "Eat, Pray, Love." I had that moment where I thought, "Ha you're sad, lonely, pathetic." Then I shifted. I laughed and enjoyed. What a different feeling it was to enjoy the time to myself, to eat what I want and watch what I want.

So many times we get stuck in judgment, feeling victim to our circumstances when all we have to do is shift to enjoyment. Is there an area in your life where you can shift, and see the story you're telling yourself in a different light? It seems we always want the other side or something else. When what matters, is finding enjoyment and peace no matter your circumstances.

Next time you feel sad, lonely, or pathetic, change your perspective. It will change everything. It will raise your energy. I promise you will feel lighter, even for a moment. Enjoy the pizza in bed, the sappy romantic comedy, and the red wine. It's exactly what you need.

What would happen if you let light and laughter come into your life in moments when you don't exactly feel that way?

First Place

I can not think of a time in my life when I got first place, I was second in the nation in gymnastics, second on my dance team, who knows what else. I think maybe I got a blue ribbon in elementary school for a hula-hoop contest, but I don't even know. This has caused some internal issues let me tell you; but I didn't even know that until I started to do the work, to realize who was I being, what crap I was telling myself. Then all a sudden, a light went off; and I thought, "Wow, I treat myself always like I am second."

This was a huge moment and one that is important to share. My belief in this has kept me from going for it, ruined relationships and probably much more than I know. I know it seems ridiculous and it was so long ago, but I believed I was second in life. It was this *belief* that was the problem.

Now I know that I am #1 and might even go buy myself a gold medal to remind myself daily. All I had to do was change my belief. What belief do you have about yourself that keeps you in second place? Does that prevent you from showing up in the world and claiming your place on the podium?

Stone

Have you ever felt like maybe, "If I turn to stone, the heart-break I feel will go away?" It makes me think of the Stone heads on Easter Island, some of them have bodies but most of them are just heads. Which is what happens to us when we turn our hearts to stone. We become just a thinking head, cut off from our true selves. We stop feeling and overthink.

I know it may be easier to try to turn it off, to turn to stone, but what you're really doing is cutting off love that wants to come your way. Lookup a picture of the Stone Heads on Easter Island, look at their faces all rigid, stuck, no move-ment, no breath, no flow. Is that really how you want to feel?

When you have a heartbreak of any kind, let the tears flow, the heart feel, allowing the healing to begin. Don't cut off the infinite supply of love we are given by turning to stone.

Wild Child

love the phrase "Wild child." I love the songs and the stories I hear about being a wild child. It's freeing, invigorating to be a "Wild child," and we all are. We just let being an adult get in the way. We forget about the fun, free, wild child side we have. We get stuck in the rat race, forget we were a child before we were an adult, and we need to let our hair blow in the wind,

The phrase "Wild child" reminds me to laugh and let go, to turn around and enjoy, to be curious and open to possibility. A wild child shares love and joy. She is free to follow her soul, her calling. We all have a wild child in us. You just have to find her again and give her permission to be wild, to enjoy.

Let go of "supposed to" and find freedom. Freedom to be you, to laugh a little more, to let your hair down in the wind. What can you do today to find your inner wild child? Let her out and let her run through the field of wildflowers.

Popcorn

Popcorn is not dinner (I'm sorry), yet when I'm cooking dinner for myself, I will make popcorn, or a frozen pizza, or something else that I would not make for guests or my family. I would never feed my loved ones popcorn for dinner, so why do I make it for myself?

Don't get me wrong, sometimes it's nice to enjoy a night off from cooking, but sometimes we make ourselves a crappy meal because we don't put ourselves first. It's important we recognize the difference here, because when we don't treat ourselves as good as we treat others, we are saying subconsciously, "I am not as important."

Take a moment to think about that. Do you treat yourself just as good as you treat others? If we don't take care of ourselves, then how can we show up for the people we love? Cooking for one is not hard, it's easy because you can make whatever you want, whatever you like and eat the leftovers at midnight. On the nights you feel like putting yourself last because you don't have someone to cook for, make your favorite meal just for you. It's worth the dishes to realize how important you are. On the nights you just want a night off from cooking, enjoy the popcorn. Do you treat yourself as well as you treat others?

Tennis Balls

I walked into my house one day to find my sweet lab pup Rosco hiding in the corner like he did something wrong. So I started the investigation process. You know--what did he eat or do that he's hiding? Come to find out, he had dug into the bag of tennis balls I use for yoga classes that I left sitting on the ground. The tennis balls were all over the house. I just started laughing, looked at him, and let him know he was not in trouble; but I loved him for being him because he simply loves tennis balls--after all they are fun to chew and chase.

Do you ever find moments in your life like that, that you love something so much, yet want to hide it? You hide what you really love, because of fear of judgment or you are not good enough to love it.

You see, Rosco loves tennis balls. He will sleep with one next to his head, ready for me to throw it at any moment. That's how much he loves them. Why do we hide who we are or what we truly love? Are we afraid someone is going to take it, laugh at us or tell us it's stupid? What is something you truly love? It's part of you. Stop hiding and let the world know you love it. You'll bring more of it into your life. Start leaving your tennis balls all over the house and love the things you love.

Game Trails

If you have ever been in nature where wild animals live, you will notice game trails. These are the trails that the animals walk on over and over. They have created a path to food, water, or to run from predators. It's the easiest path. Just as the animals do, we have created paths in our brains that are easy to be on, and walk them over and over. Habits.

Repeating the same, low-level belief or story over and over. Now you created an easy path to stay on and blazing a trail is hard work. This is how we find ourselves stuck, by staying on the same trail.

Trust me, I have all kinds of trails that I am working on, I'm cutting a new path, a new way of thinking. The new trails are filled with love, positive affirmations, and I must keep blazing ahead. Otherwise, we find ourselves not forging ahead, but taking the easy path.

What is a new trail you can start to carve into your brain today? How about the trail of I am peace, I am enough, I am successful. Or the path that all your dreams come true? Choose one path and blaze ahead. You'll notice your whole world will change, just by changing your thoughts. You'll have a new trail that leads you to your dreams.

Aspen Trees

One of the world's largest living organisms is an Aspen Grove in Utah. It has over 47,000 trees but shares one root system. I believe this is amazing and that together, they thrive. Individually they might be good, but not thrive. If we let nature teach us here, we can very clearly see the lesson.

Together we are better, stronger and can battle the storms. Women need women. Men need men. Women need Men. Men need Women. We have a special connection, a special root system. It's time we stop belittling each other and grow together, with one root system. This is why we have each other; we are not meant to weather the storm alone. It's why taking time to nurture your relationships; your friendships are key to thriving we are better together.

We help each other stand when the storm blows through, when the rains come in and when the lightning strikes. Are you allowing others to help you, to work with one root system, or are you trying to stand all on your own?

Jacket

We all have been in this chapter, no matter at what age. Where his damn hoodie or jacket is still at your house. Do I let him know? Do I burn it? Am I pathetic if I sleep in it? The list goes on. First, you are enough without him. SAY THAT AGAIN.

Second it sucks and hurts like hell. Sometimes it feels like it will never go away. It will. This too shall pass. Remember you are a Superwoman. Lift your head.

So many times, we fight the pain instead of feeling it. Feeling it sucks. No matter if it is from a breakup, a job, a loss. Feeling it is hard. But I have learned that feeling, moves you through. Sitting in it feels like it will always feel that way, but I promise you it won't. Let it flow over you, then rinse it off and step into the badass woman you are.

Feeling, releases it. Lets it go. Feeling, creates a space for you to heal and move beyond your past. Is there something you just need to feel, to release? How can you create space today by feeling it and then saying, "Ok, next?

The Zipper

M y mom's nickname in high school was the zipper. People used to say that If she turned sideways and stuck out her tongue she was so little and flat she looked like a zipper. Now, she is beautiful; but let's just say no longer flat-chested (I hope she doesn't kill me for writing this). I share this story with you because all of our bodies change. Has yours?

The thing is here we forget all the stories that come with the changes, like how your body got you through all those games you played as a kid, or how it helped you make the sports team, or maybe your hands painted beautiful art. Your body got you through those rough nights in college or the birth of your beautiful babies. What about those laugh lines or those crows feet of wisdom. I think they should be called owl lines because they are signs of being wise.

No matter how your body has changed, love it, acknowledge it, and have gratitude for it. You will only have one. Shift your perspective of your body to love, gratitude, and stories, it will change your entire life.

The Trailer

I got a new horse trailer and was so excited to use it until one of my horses, Waylon, would not get into it. He was scared, uncertain, and couldn't see the big picture. He didn't know it was just a new trailer, and I wasn't taking him from his friends or locking him in a scary box on wheels. He just didn't know what was happening next.

Do you ever feel that way? Like if you could only see what was going to happen next you would get in the trailer, you would take the leap? If Waylon had known we were going to a super fun horse expo, that the trailer was safe, and I was bringing him back to his buddies, I bet he would have gotten in with ease-instead of spending 3 hours refusing to enter (That's another story). We tend to do this in life. We don't take the next step because we don't know what's going to happen.

Here's the thing, you are never going to know the future, and you will never know what is going to happen. So why hold back why not take the leap and go for the ride? Get into the trailer and trust.

The Trailer Part 2

There are all kinds of tricks and tools you can use to get your horse in a trailer, but this one particular morning, my horse would not load. I did not have time for that. I needed him in the trailer now.

Do you ever feel like when you need something done, now is the exact time everything goes wrong? The exact time the universe says, "I have a different plan."

Honestly, at this point in my life, I believe it's a constant lesson in patience and control. I'm still not sure which one I need more of, a lesson in patience, or one that I am not in control of. I never got him in the trailer and ended up sitting in the trailer in tears, frustrated, angry, and annoyed, feeling defeated.

After a day that 100% did not go as planned, I knew it was because there was a bigger plan. God had a different plan for me that day, and it was perfect. Sometimes the things we find as inconvenient and frustrating are actually perfectly orchestrated, perfectly created for you. Are you trying to control you or the situation?

Scars

One of my best friends tells her kids when they get bumps and bruises, "It's okay. Scars are stories." I have heard her say it for 10 years or so, and I always love it when she does. How many scars do you have that are filled with stories? I think so many times we believe scars are bad, ugly or remind of us painful times.

What if scars remind you of how strong you are, and how your body healed? What if scars remind you that you are perfect as you are because they are all part of your story? That's the key. Scars are not your story. They are part of it. It's living with grit and grace. They will never go away, and they don't need to. Why would you want to get rid of who you are, what has made you, and how all your experiences have made you the Superwoman you are today?

So no matter how many scars you have, where they are, or what they are from, they are beautiful and make you, you. What's better than being you, scars and all?

Rip to Heal

When you are building muscle, fibers in the muscle rip in order to grow. The heart is a muscle, and for it to grow, it rips as well. It's painful. It's sore. It takes time to heal. It's hard, but remember your heart is growing.

That is the beautiful part. In your heartache, in your torment, your heart is growing to love more. So many of us go the other way after heartbreak. We shut down. We build a wall so no one can ever hurt us again. Have you ever noticed how that causes more pain? That is because it goes against what the body and heart want to do naturally, which is love and be loved.

I know that in the moment, it feels like the pain is never going to go away, but if you remember your heart is ripping to be able to love more, the healing process will become easier, lighter. Give yourself time to heal. That is how you come back stronger and able to love more. Allow the body to heal. Don't force the healing process. In the long run, it's like putting a bandaid on a broken leg. Give it the proper time and attention it deserves. No matter where you are in life, is there a part of your heart you need to heal?

Snakes

I hate snakes with a passion. They slither in. They find the cracks, the weaknesses, they can climb walls and have no legs. Seriously? They are a lot like jealousy, fear, hate, anger, ego and just simply put, the devil. I also know they help out with mice and spiders, so we need them. They are, unfortunately, a part of the perfect cycle of nature. This is why self-love, loving friendships, and relationships are so important because it helps keep the snakes away.

Snakes will slither fast into the weaknesses. When we take care of ourselves, live by faith in the universe, meditate, pray, and spread love, those snakes can't find the cracks as quickly or sometimes ever. We can fight them off with kindness instead of feeling like we have to come at them as a raging force or running away with high knees like I do. We can look them in the face and say, "Not today. Today, no matter what, I choose peace, joy, love, and kindness."

Do you have cracks you need to fill to keep the snakes away? Cracks of jealousy, hate, revenge? Snakes thrive on those emotions. Cancel your plans with the snakes, with the devil. You've got work to do.

Sharks

I read that if you put a shark in an 8-inch fishbowl, it will grow to be 8 inches, if you put the shark in the ocean, it will grow to be 8 feet long. The moral is, who are you surrounding yourself with? Are they helping you grow or restricting you?

My question is, who is putting a shark in an 8-inch fishbowl in the first place? The answer to that question is, you did. Or I did. Sometimes we create our own imaginary glass bowl.

Why do we create this imaginary 8-inch glass ball around us that we have to break, to fight to get out of to survive? It's not who you are meant to be. You are powerful, beautiful, and alive. You are not intended to be in an 8-inch fishbowl but living, thriving and sharing your strengths with the world.

Get out of the fishbowl and thrive. It's your God-given destiny. How big is your glass bowl? Break free. Now it's time to get rid of it once and for all and swim in the vast ocean.

Superglue

There is a really old folktale I called "The Tar Baby" which is an excellent example of how we get ourselves into messes. In the tale, Br'er Fox dresses up a doll and rolls it in tar in order to try and catch Br'er Rabbit. Well, the rabbit comes along and gets no response from the doll. He then gets upset and punches the doll, getting stuck to the tar, then kicks the doll. The more rage he has, the worse he gets stuck.

Ok, for real, I just laughed at this story when I heard it, because I don't know how many times I have thought, "Oh, I can fix this," just to find myself in a modern version of the story and superglued to the floor allowing my emotions and desire to control to take over as compared to stepping back and asking God for guidance. These are the moments where stopping, breathing and allowing yourself a moment are going to keep you (and me) from getting stuck.

How many times have you been like Rabbit and get yourself stuck, worse off than when you started? Seriously, stop. This is the best reminder that God does not need our help. That he is capable of handling it. Our job is to trust and let go, so we don't find ourselves superglued to the problem. How often do you find yourself in a situation where just stopping would have been the best option?

First Aid Kit

Do you carry around your version of a first aid kit, ready to repair anything the second something could go wrong? (Sometimes my first aid kit is whiskey and duck tape) Does the phrase, "What if there is nothing wrong," make you freeze in your tracks? How can it be? What if we keep thinking this because we have programmed ourselves to believe this?

I think this concept is so foreign to us because even in the moments when nothing is wrong, we are so used to mothering or feeling the need to fix something, that we create a problem where there is no problem. I am so guilty, but yet I am realizing, there is nothing wrong.

It is okay. Everything is okay. Most of the time, it is more than okay. It's good, so are you creating a problem where there is no problem? Instead of wanting to fix everything, you can sit down and take a break because there is nothing to fix. You are not broken, you never have been. Maybe you have times where you feel like you're not going to get through, but just ride that wave out and let it go. It's carrying that on our back which creates more drama. Nothing is wrong; nothing is wrong with what you do, who you are, where you've been, where you're going. You do not need to continually carry a first aid kit around, ready to repair something at the first sign up an accident. Set down your first aid kit, enjoy the lightness. Ask yourself, "What if nothing is wrong?"

Some Time

A good friend of mine had just broken up with her partner of 3 years, and I asked how she was. She's a tough one, and I knew I wasn't gonna get much of answer. The answer I did get was empowering.

She said, "I'm fine. I am going to give myself a month and then move on." I know there are so many things that can go into that, but what I want to share is, she was allowed. She knew she was going to need some time. Time to heal, to think, to breathe, and she gave herself permission.

I think that is the challenge, allowing yourself some time to heal. We all function on different timelines, and hers was a month. For some people, that time is a week; some a month; some longer. No matter what it is, when there is a loss in our life, we all need time to heal. Think about it like this, if you went and broke your leg, you're not going to run a marathon the next day. Well, the heart is a muscle. It needs time to heal also. No matter what it is, give yourself permission to breathe and rest. Know that it is going to help you in the long run because then the body can repair correctly instead of rushing the process.

Do you need to give yourself permission today to let your body and soul heal?

The Sweet Stuff

I don't mean candy here, I mean the moments where we stop enjoying the joy. The sweet stuff that is right in front of us. Candy does play a part here because one of the reasons we eat more cake and candy is because of what sugar does to the brain. It literally is like a drug which is why we keep going back for more sweets.

With that said, if we notice the joy in front of us, having gratitude for what we have, it will keep coming back to us. We will spread joy, and then more will be produced. Just like candy, we will crave the giving of joy. This will produce more joy, it's a universal law.

Take a moment today and write down three small things that bring you joy. Then start doing them every day. Keep those in your routine no matter how small they are. Then add to your list. Keep it going, and any time you need to remind yourself of all the joy in front of you stop and give thanks. Notice how this starts to change your life just by taking the time to notice the joy in front of you, the warm cup of coffee, the phone call from a friend, the way your puppy looks at you. You'll start to create more joy the second you shift your attention to how much joy is right in front of you. The sweet stuff, how can you notice it today?

Puzzle Pieces

The goal of the puzzle is to piece it together into one beautiful picture. I have seen some puzzles framed, but for the most part when they are done, they are broken up into little pieces and put back in the box.

Do you ever feel like you are breaking pieces of you off to fit into someone else's mold, saying, "Okay, that part of me can go." Just to find that eventually, you feel broken into so many pieces you don't know who you are? You were not meant to live in a puzzle box. You were meant to be out in the open and framed for sure.

Why do we do this, allow parts of us to go so we can fit into a mold? You made the mold, then it was broken. Just like my mold and everyone else you know, there is one mold per person. If you feel as if you have put pieces of you into a box to hide them, go get your puzzle box and put your whole self back together. You are perfect whole; even the parts of you feel like you have to hide. If you have ever put a 1000 piece puzzle together to get to the end and have one piece missing, it feels incomplete almost pointless. Just as you need every piece to be complete. Think about that, and who you are. Whole, you are beautiful, strong and most importantly complete. Are there pieces of you that you shoved in a box, pieces of you that you need to feel whole again?

Relax and Breathe

One time I got told to relax and breathe, to stop being dramatic in a conversation. Let's just say, I was not stoked. It was like that perfect girl moment of, "I can't believe he said that." I was just baffled. I called a girlfriend, poured a glass of wine said, "I can't believe he said that." I thought there was no way I was wrong, no way did I need to relax and breathe. Of course, she agreed, I was not any of these things.

Then a few days later, I thought, what if I do relax and breathe? What if that's all I need to do? I need to stop trying to figure out what's going to happen. Stop trying to control the situation, in this case the relationship, the future. I thought because I didn't overreact, what I said was nice, it was calm, I was just sharing how I was feeling, that I was right.

The problem was my intention was controlling without even realizing it, I wanted to control the future. Sharing how you feel is valid, important and should not be discredited. The reason you are sharing how you're feeling is, I think, where we can get off track. We climb on our high horse to validate our feelings, and then word vomit them all out.

What if we took the time to breathe and relax before we have convinced ourselves we are right? The "breathe and re-lax" comes before we create the story or the fight that doesn't exist. Enjoying the time to breathe will always lead to the best outcome. Take a minute to call your girlfriend. Let it out; but ultimately take a breath. If it circles back around, again and again, address your feelings, but from a place of love and calmness, not control and fear. I promise you won't regret it. It's way better than the other way, than doing or saying something you regret. Next time you get told to breathe and relax, try it out. It might be some of the best advice you have ever gotten.

Doing Dishes

Do you ever have the pan that you scrub and scrub, but you know to get it clean you just need to let it soak, to stop trying so hard? I think there is a life lesson for us here, to stop trying so hard. I know that goes against all you know, but leave the dish. Let it soak. Stop breaking a sweat trying to scrub it.

We have heard this so many ways, dig-in, keep going, keep scrubbing, do more. Has this ever really worked? When has something forced ever really worked out? Start working from a place of what drives you, who are you truly and allow the flow to happen. When you follow the path designed for you, your natural path will become effortless. You will draw in your own authentic experiences, people, and desires when you stop forcing things to happen.

Your natural abilities will come through your heart's natural desires. I don't mind doing the dishes, but spending more time on them than I need? Well, that just seems stupid. I can let it soak; I can stop trying to scrub hard enough to get it clean when all is need is a little soap, water, and time. Then just like that, it was easy and effortless because I allowed the process to happen. How can you stop trying so hard today and allow your natural path to unfold?

Ocean Money

I had an excellent opportunity to lead a group of women to Costa Rica for a yoga retreat. It was a week of letting go, learning and relaxation. One of the days, we were relaxing in the ocean just talking, when all of a sudden, some money floated over to me. It was 1000 Colones, equivalent to about $2 dollars US.

The first thing was the exciting feeling of having money flow right to me especially because I happened to be reading the book, <u>Dollars Flow to Me Easily</u> (great book, I recommend it.). Then the logical, overthinking side left side of the brain said, "Who cares? It's $2 bucks."

I never spent the money on the trip, and now it's on my desk as a reminder that when we are open to the flow of the universe and thankful for the smallest things, this is where the magic happens. That $2 was way more than money. It was a reminder that when we feel good, that's when things flow.

Money, love, abundance, they start to appear out of the deep blue. It's the overthinking, not noticing the small signs in the big picture we miss. Yes, I wanted more than $2 bucks to flow to me that day, but that wasn't the point. The lesson was to let it flow, be open, and be thankful. Are you open and grateful for ocean money or are you saying who cares it was only $2?

Serving Heart

Recently I had to call a customer service number to make changes to my car insurance. I dialed the number, completely expecting this was going to be a pain, and the tone of my voice showed it. I was expecting poor service. You know, we have all had that experience where the customer service was not the best or didn't meet our expectations. I bet most of the time, we matched their vibe right back. At least I know I have several times and was starting to do it at this particular time.

"Well, fine. You're gonna be rude to me? I'll be rude right back," has often been my thinking. Let's stop for a brief second. What if on that day the customer service person has a sick kid? Maybe they are fighting with their partner, or their bills are late, or what if there is something going on we know nothing about? Or maybe they weren't rude and you were just expecting rudeness?

I am not saying that poor service is justifiable. I am saying, however, what if you can be the light they need that day? Instead of matching their vibe, lift yours and be the person that makes their day better.

It's important to remember they are doing their best, and that is different from yours. When we mirror back a crappy attitude, all we do is take our day down. We leave the restaurant, hotel, or wherever, and then complain about the crappy service to someone else. How is that helping anyone? As a Superwoman, you have a serving heart. Let's spread that love around a little more. You never know when your smile, your kindness, your extra tip just makes someone's day, that little action is all they needed. How can you be the light today?

Really Dream

Why are so many of us afraid to really dream? Like really dream! Far bigger than you could ever imagine, if you can imagine it's possible. Could you imagine what could come true? When I think about this question what stops me is the fear of not being deserving or yeah right that could never happen to me. But it can, it will and the same goes for your dreams. I am more deserving and more importantly God wants to give it to me. He wants to give you your deepest wildest desires, hopes and dreams. We just have to be open and believe in the worthiness of receiving. Think about how many times you have gone to lunch and someone else picks up the check, to just argue over who is really going to pay. You are refusing a gift, and as I have learned, when it's a gift you don't get a choice if you want it or not. It's a gift. Receiving is just as important as giving, it's allowing yourself to be given a gift of any magnitude. Receive with gratitude, peace, a full heart and enjoy as your dreams start to unfold. Close your eyes and tap into that warm fuzzy feeling of no limit dreams, let yourself not just imagine but living the life you want, fully step into it. Be open to the good. See your life as you want it to be, not as it is. Are you open to the good or is it too good to be true? Nothing is.

Real love

I have always loved love. I love going deep with people, connecting and showing them I love them. I have also found myself heartbroken and wondering how I can love something that hurts me so much. Then I got wiser and the breakthrough happened, I loved love but I didn't really love me. Even though I thought I did, I was my own worst critic. I hated my mistakes, my failures, I never thought I was pretty enough, smart enough, good enough, among all the other stories I have told myself. I thought that is how people know me, for the things I did supposedly wrong. But how could I find love, or have anyone love me back when I didn't love me?

Now, sometimes, those stories creep back in, but I know they are lies. They were never failures only lessons That's where the real love is when you love every part of yourself when you give yourself grace and can laugh at yourself. When you love every so-called mistake, failure, set back, every tear, and every moment that makes you, you. When I love someone, I love all of them. Even the things that might drive me crazy. Love yourself like that, even the things that drive you insane. Loving yourself first that's what real love is. Do you really love your whole self?

3 Amazing Women

Two of my girlfriends and I were having a good ol girls night and the usual conversations, life, work, men, horseback riding, men. Each of us at this time was some form of upset or frustrated with our partners, whom we all love dearly. But as I sat there and listened to us talk I couldn't help but wonder why do we give so much of ourselves to men and forget how amazing we are. My girlfriends are wonderful, beautiful, talented, successful badass women.

Yet I think we tend to forget that time and time again or maybe we don't tell each other enough. What it made me realize, is we all go through it and why we need to build each other up, that's why girlfriends are so important. We can share stores, relate and remember we are so different from men. We process differently. We need to talk through things, cry and laugh about life and it's so much sweeter together. Reminding each other that we hold our own power and self-love. Remembering that self-love and confidence do not come from a man but from inside. To remember we are all amazing, and that it is ok to laugh at silly boys. Do you know how amazing you are?

Escape Artist

M an, I thought I had this one mastered, then realized I was hurting myself and my gift to the world. I have escaped from showing up in the world because of fear of judgment, fear of not good enough, fear of failure, whatever it may be. I found a way to escape. Like a regular ol' Houdini. I would find a way to study something, I would clean the house, go to the grocery store on the other side of town to escape. I would hide from writing this book, creating a coaching package or launching an avenue of my business. To finally realize there is nowhere to escape to because it would find me.

The drive to help others, to show up in the world that drive is deep within and won't go away. There is no escaping what is deep within you. Now there is no more escaping because I realized I wasn't hurting myself but others, those that needed to hear my story or my coaching so they could relate and grow too. Your story, is someone else's handbook. It will help them connect no matter what you do for work or life. Let go of being an escape artist because your true self will always find you and push you out of hiding. You are meant to light up the world not escape from it. What ways are you hiding, how can you stop escaping?

Cowboys and Indians

There is a wonderful quote by Wayne Dyer that says "If you knew who walked beside you at all times you would never experience fear or doubt again" He is talking about your guides, spirits, angels. I find so much comfort in that quote, knowing that I am never alone. Two of my guides have always been an Indian and a Cowboy. The old wise kind that gives me the tough love I need as well as so much comfort. It's like when I was a kid I had an imaginary friend, now as an adult I have guides and angels, same thing now just a grown-up name.

Can you imagine your guides next to you, what do they look like, what does it feel like to know they are there? I love my cowboy and Indian they remind me to be playful just as the game we played as kids, running around using our imagination, creating anything we wanted. This is called manifestation as you get older, but now we have so much attachment; we forget to have fun and relax allowing our guide team to do their job. I have sat down in a field and had a full conversation with my cowboy, he's old, wise and knows so much more than I do, he reminds me to play the game of life just as I did as a kid. Who are your guides, can you ask them for guidance, letting go if that sounds crazy and have fun with your imagination?

Green Grass

How many times have you wanted the greener grass, only to find out you would rather go back to where you were? So many times, we find ourselves hoping for the other thing, that we are missing what is right in front of us, or enjoying the phase of life we are in. We want the relationship so bad, we don't enjoy we have the whole bed to ourselves, we hope for the bigger house to find it is much harder to clean, whatever it may be we are missing the green grass right in front of us. If we keep looking to the other side of the fence, we will miss our whole lives. Next thing we know we will wonder where all the time has gone because we are always looking for the next thing. Slow down, be grateful, look at how good it really is right in front of you. All it takes is just a mind shift, to realize the grass is greener where you water it. Start to notice all the beauty in front of you now, like this very second the wonderful food you have, the body that takes you places the roof over your head. Maybe your not exactly where you want to be but when you start to water the grass in front of you, you will feel the shifts the growth, you will be able to live for today.

Nikki Glandon

Little Girl

Would you ever walk up to a friend and say, "Girl, you are not good enough, you're too fat, too skinny, ugly, not smart enough, you're a failure." So why do we do that when we look in the mirror when we talk to ourselves? I've gotten better at the negative self chatter, but it creeps in, and I just remember it's the little girl inside me screaming for attention.

We all of some version of the little girl inside us, it's letting her know everything is ok that is key. Sometimes she throws temper tantrums and feeds you the not good enough lies. Allowing her to stay is all she wants, she wants to know she is safe, loved, and protected. Tell her she is, let her show up and then tell her to take a seat because you are strong, wonderful, beautiful and confident. Talk to her like you would dear friend with nothing but loving words. She is part of you, your life has made you who you are today and the pieces of you that you may want to get rid of, make you, you. So make friends with all the pieces of you, that little girl inside of you that was chosen last for kickball or made fun of letting her know she is all good. Become your own best friend. Try out writing yourself a letter like you would your best friend, then believe it!

Spirit Animal

My girlfriend loves Sloths, not in the crazy creepy way, more in the way that she thinks they are great fun animals that have this sneaky smile. When I found this out I cracked up, because she isn't a sloth type person. She is always going, doing and hustling, she is always lighting up the party and having a blast. I love her and realizing she loved sloths so much, made me know her even better. See, the sloth is her spirit animal because it's this side of her that unless you know her, you won't see. It is part of her true spirit, of who she is.

Is there a side of you that only a few people see your true spirit animal or is it completely hiding? This side of you is special, intimate and lets people in, once all parts of you are known. Maybe your spirit animal is a bird and you crave to fly, but yet don't let yourself because you once were told you couldn't. Are you a monkey, playful and want to swing from branch to branch, yet have to be serious as an adult?

If you choose right now, what animal is deep within that is ready to get out to fly free, to dive deep? Let those close you know you, really know you. Be free from the cage and let all parts of you shine through, embrace that maybe one day your a tiger and somedays your a sloth, tap into your calling your true spirit animal. What is your spirit animal?

Beachball

Have you ever noticed what happens when you shove a beachball underwater? It bursts through the surface with a lot of velocity. Have you ever noticed that happening with how you feel? So many times this is what we do with our feelings, we shove them down and expect to go away, only for them to show up like a beachball bursting from the water with no control. Then the next thing you know, you're a madwoman over spilt milk, the people involved wondering what in the world is wrong. Maybe you get the oh so favorite question "Is it that time of the month? When the truth is you have shoved your emotions all down so far that it's uncontrollable.

Think about a beach volleyball game, you have control over that ball, you see where it's at and what it's doing. Next time you find yourself burying your feelings down see what happens when you can control them just like you can in the volleyball game. Yes, you can control them and when you do you won't explode over the small things. Ask yourself is this one I can let go of or am I shoving it down to avoid it? Trust yourself enough to share how you feel, the key is learning to do it with control.

Fearless

My mom and I were on horses recently and working with a new equine coach who called my mom, "fearless" as an insult, or in a negative context, let's just say.

I was confused as to how the word "fearless" could become an insult, and also thought I love to be called "fearless." I wish sometimes I was more fearless. Then I realized it's not a negative, that we should all be fearless, to be willing to try, to go for, it to be brave.

That is exactly what was happening in this story, my mom was going for it. She was willing to try, to say, "Yes" and be fearless. It was beautiful and encouraging. I love that my 65-year-old mother was called "fearless," that she knows how to live and experience. What a blessing to be called fearless.

She is an example of how to live, how to enjoy the present moment and all the opportunities in front of her. So the next time someone wants to insult you because of their own fear, show them what it's really like to be fearless. Show them how to really live. How can you be fearless today?

Trust Yourself

If you trusted yourself what would you do right now? This has to be one of the best questions my coach ever asked me. See I wasn't trusting myself, I don't think I even knew what that question meant. I thought I did, trust myself but deep down I trusted myself on the small things but not the big things. I trusted I could make a good meal, or teach a great yoga class, but I wasn't trusting myself to make the right decisions in the big areas of my life. I kept looking to externally circumstances when I need to make a choice. I would phone a friend, call my mom, pray, and yes that is how we get answers and work through things, but I wanted them to tell me what to do instead of talk through it.

So many times we already know the answer but don't trust ourselves enough to do it. Have you been told that before, the phrase "You know what to do"? You're being told that because you do. We have the answers right inside of us, your body will tell you, you know deep down what is your truth. Can you imagine how many unwanted situations you could have avoided by trusting yourself. This all circles back to knowing yourself and truly loving all parts of you. Start trusting yourself, follow your gut, it knows what it is doing. Can you get still today and listen to your inner voice? Do you trust yourself?

Overtaking

While I was writing the other day I went to type the word overthinking. Auto-correct, for some reason, changed it to overtaking. It blew my mind because that is exactly what overthinking is. It's your logical left brain trying to think it's way out of a problem or situation, its the ego trying to "keep you safe" it's overtaking your mind. It comes in hot and heavy taking over what you truly know, making you believe all the stories you've created in your head. It's like a hostile takeover, not willing to let the grip go until you surrender and give up. Don't give up.

Letting overthinking turn into overtaking is just another sneaky way that the enemy slides in, wanting you play it small, instead of light up the world. I can say my brain has been overtaking before by awful thoughts and stories to make me wonder who's brain is this, to realize I am in charge of my thoughts and my own brain the enemy does not win this battle. Feed the brain good thoughts, that is the strength you need and you have it. Not to be strong in adversity but strong in what you tell yourself. Don't turn overthinking, into overtaking.

Impact

There are so many things in our lives that create impact, good and bad. So things impact us so much we lose our path and get knocked off course, some things impact our life's purpose and meaning. The impact is powerful and can create change, it is a way to create movement. Think about a jackhammer when it hits concrete the impact it makes breaks it apart into small chunks so we can move it and create something new. Sometimes situations in life may feel like you are being broken into small pieces and the impact feels devastating. There is beauty in this as it is creating way for something new to enter your life. Impact is something that affects you, it is not negative, it's what you take away from the impact that is going to set you apart.

Another way to look at this is what impact are you making in the world, are you bulldozing everything and everyone that comes into your life. Or is your impact, love, gratitude and kindness. Every day we get to choose what kind of impact to make, you get to choose how impact guides you. How are you impacting people today?

Compliments

Is there something people always compliment you about, you're a good hugger, they love how you dress, you're a great cook, you're always on time? These are your power lanes, the things you are good at, that you may not even notice. They are guides to your true self. So stop blowing them off like they are no big deal, these compliments are real and people mean them. It's a way for you see what your passions are where you may not even notice. Like the "you're a good cook" compliment, do you have a desire to cook for others, more than just at your house, like you want to write a cookbook and just think oh I can't? Are you always on time, trust me that's a gift, and people know they can count on you?

Compliments are little ways to brighten your day but also set you on your path, little clues of your true self. Sometimes it is hard to receive compliments but allow them in, and start to notice how they correlate with what you do and how you live your life. What is your favorite compliment, how does it drive you in life?

Hat Pin

had a hat pin designed when I was leading a yoga retreat in Costa Rica. It's one-of-a-kind and was designed for me. It's filled with feathers and beautiful stones. It's magical. I realized that I was a person that owns a hat pin, and I felt old but yet wise. I realized the kind of women that own hat pins are strong, wise women.

Grandmas have hatpins. I realized I was no longer a kid, I am a wise woman and I have a lot to share with the world. My stories have helped me grow to be the person I am. I think sometimes we let our stories, our growth, our changes hold us back instead of driving us forward. They become a curse, not a blessing.

All of your stories, your journeys, they are to teach you, to drive you and help you become the wise woman you are. You have more to give than you know. Your stories are your magic. When I put my hatpin on, I feel like I can do anything, it's like my version of a Superwoman cape. I tap into the wisdom of the women in the world who have seen it all, been through it all. I feel like I can fly. The truth is, I don't need a magical hat pin for that, it's always lived in me, and it lives in you. Your stories make you wise, not weak; sometimes we just need reminders that we are magical and wise. What is your version of a hat pin that brings you magic?

Alone

What is something that scares you, not like bugs or snakes but the thing in your core that scares you. Mine is being alone, not finding the love I desire in life, or finding it and losing it. What's so crazy is I am not alone, even when I am single. But that fear of being alone makes me push away my partner. I find ways to be alone just to make sure I'm ok if I'm gonna be alone. I have no idea where this fear comes from, and I know its a lie. I find myself self-sabotaging to prove a damn point, then I feel like, well why did you do that? I never prove my point.

This is what fear does it drives us to believe things that are not true and then sometimes take actions that we regret. Here's the thing I am not alone, I never have been, you never are either. I guarantee whatever silly fear you have made yourself believe comes from this place of fear and it's time for fear to take a hike. Your life is more magical than what fear does, and when you notice how it sneaks in you can start to rewire your brain and come up with your new belief. By even sharing your fear, you will start to see how silly it is, that is made up and holding you back from the life of your dreams. Whatever your silly fear is, it's time you let it go, time to stop telling yourself lies. Can you look at your fear and laugh, its the best medicine out there?

Angel Babies

I have had two miscarriages and they both sucked. I remember trying to be ok, to understand the science behind it, to do all the positive things when finally a friend said in these exact words, "it's ok for it to just fucking suck." I felt relief; someone gave me permission to feel how I really felt. It did, it just sucked, and if you have been through it you know that while it is emotionally awful its also painful it's like this double whammy.

Times like these are when you really realize you're Superwomen and this will pass, whatever kind of loss it is. In loss and grief it's easy to feel as if it is never going pass like this will always suck. It will pass, and there is relief. Now I have two angel babies they fly high above and guide me, they knew it was better to be angels than to walk on earth. It was allowing the grief, the pain to move through me that gave the babies the wings to fly. I allowed it to just fucking suck.

As Superwomen, it's hard to allow it to suck, to surrender to the grief and pain but is necessary to help you fly. You learn more compassion for others when you are able to move through your losses. I was able to help a dear friend of mine though her miscarriage because of mine, she knew she could call and I would be able to hold her hand through the loss.

Remember, if you are in a loss of any kind, it will pass and your story will help someone else. Sometimes you get more angels to guide you through life. What losses do you have that are now your own version of angels?

Soulfight

I just love this word, soulfight. It feels powerful, sexy, and something I want to sign up for. A soulfight? I'm in. I heard it in a song and realized how powerful it is. Fighting for your soul, what other battles would you rather fight, besides the desires of your soul? Your soul is your life force it's what drives your life, your choices, your hopes, your dreams. Your soul is what passes on after death it's your essence.

So a soul fight is your mission, it's acknowledging what your soul says and then fighting for it. I am not talking about like a bad fight but the beautiful dance with life to honor what your soul craves. This takes some quite some time, some scary leaps of faith and listening to your inner voice, your soul. What else out there is more important to fight for besides your own soul? Stop the outside battle with the world, drop the should, the worry of judgment and start your soulfight now. If you don't fight for what your soul says who else will? Start your soulfight today.

Happier

I remember having a lingering sickness one winter. The kind of sick you can work through, but not at 100%. I kept fighting it and I didn't want to go to the doctor. Until I finally realized, man, I would love to feel 100%. I went to the doctor and a week later was good to go. The point is how many times do we stay in a job, relationship or situation that is not 100%. There are ebbs and flows in everything but I'm talking about the times you know you're not 100% happy. What would it feel like to be happier? To finally get the courage to say I want 100% happiness, not just 90%. That's the crazy part is 90% is good, but what would it feel like to be 100% happy? To know that you can have that.

Instead so often we cut or selves short, thinking well this is good, I can function here, nothing is wrong. It's like the cold, you can keep going to work, be a mom, go to the easy yoga class but you know that 10% is missing, you know you could be thriving. That leap is scary and it takes courage to walk away from something the gives you ok happiness. To me that's the momentum I want, because I know I am deserving of 100% happiness. Do you know you are worthy and deserving of 100% happiness, how can you start working towards that today?

Stained Glass

Growing up, my dad made stained glass pieces. They are beautiful, and I love stained glass. They come in so many designs, colors, sizes, and are beautiful pieces of art. I love when you walk into an old church, filled with stained glass, that smells of ancient wood and you feel the power of all the prayer that has happened in that church, then the light shines through and creates a feeling of warmth and comfort.

What I love about these beautiful pieces of art is that they are made from broken pieces of glass put together to make beautiful whole pieces of art. I love thinking about myself as a beautiful piece of stained glass, made from pieces of broken glass and perfectly put together to let the light shine through. You are art and life is art, sometimes we get to busy to notice the beauty in it all. To notice the beauty in yourself, to allow the light to shine through.

We constantly feel as if we have to keep fixing instead of realizing you are beautiful and made from all colors of broken glass. No stained glass is the same, every piece every part of you is perfectly put together to let the light shine through. You are art and just like stained glass, there is only one you. How can you let the light shine through today?

Chicken Wings

The phrase people don't change really tends to blow my mind. Are you the same person you were 2 years ago, 6 months ago, yesterday? We change all the time, we find new hobbies, new foods we like, things we no longer like. The only thing that stays the same is change. It's how you move through change that is going to impact your life. Change brings growth, new adventures, and people into your life. The thing about change is the only thing you can control is how you change. We have to stop trying to change others and take care of our growth our shifts. Years ago I didn't like chicken wings; now I do because I finally found some that aren't gross; Sometimes it's the small things. I wasn't an author 6 months ago, now I am. Sometimes it's the big things. I think change is the driving force behind creativity, life and how you are meant to show up in the world. Change closes doors and opens doors, change keeps us unstuck. How have you changed, from the small things to the big things? Allow change to be good not scary and your ride on this planet will be much more enjoyable.

Nikki Glandon

Rockstar

—

It is opening night; the stage is set, it's time for your show! Do you find yourself being the lead singer, drummer and backup dancer when your favorite song comes on? That's because you are a rockstar! Singing and dancing are a way to let stuck energy out, so girl, embrace your inner rockstar.

Take a moment and think about your perfect concert, what does the stage look like, is there a light show, what are you wearing? Now turn up the music and embrace your inner rockstar. Your life is the concert; it's your show. When are you going to be the lead singer in your own show? It's easy to keep waiting, waiting for the perfect stage, band and backup dancers. If you keep waiting, you'll find yourself just waiting. Go for your perfect concert, go for the light show and what sets your soul free, let your show sell out. Come up with your stage name and rock it. Let your hair down and get out your air guitar because its time for you to take the stage. Your show is sold out, the curtain is up and the stage is set. The only thing that's holding the show up is you. What concert are you giving?

Magic Wand

Ok, I have to admit it would be nice if I had a magic wand and could control other people's behaviors. But I don't. I could definitely say I like to be in control; most of us do even when we say we don't. This is one of the biggest lessons I have ever learned, that I am not in control, or at least there is very little I can control. But I for sure can not control other people's behaviors or choices. That is a hard pill to swallow because so many times I want to wave my magic wand and bam make them do what I think or want.

When you learn this lesson, your whole world will change. You will find freedom in your choices and choose things for you, not other people. How freeing is that? You can't control other people, so you can let that worry go. You can allow yourself choices that are best for you and your soul. You will see what really fills you up and brightens your day. You may notice your worry subsides because it's not your job to control other people's choices. It's your job to show up the best you can for the world, and that happens when you take care of the choices that work best for you.

When you let go of control the situation will change because you changed, and that's all you can control. Ok admit it, are you a control freak, or do you control only you?

Goddess

I love this word, and I love to embrace myself as a goddess. You are as well, did you know that? We allow too many people to take this from us, rob us of our internal goddess. She sits right in your soul and is dressed in robes and jewels that are beautiful and eloquent. Can you embrace her, can you let her shine through?

You no longer have to hide the warrior goddess in you, set her free. A goddess knows the respect she deserves, and shares her gifts with the world. She stands tall and proud, leads the way. She is also soft, kind and gentle. Do you treat yourself like a goddess or do you dim your light? I have this one flowing robe that makes me feel like I stepped out of Egypt when I put it on, I know there is no way I am not a goddess. Sometimes we need little reminders to step back into goddess mentality, like a flowy robe or a beautiful piece of jewelry. You don't need a special occasion to wear it, put it on today, and instantly see yourself as the beautiful goddess you are.

Asking Too Much

Do you think that sometimes, you're just asking too much, in life, a relationship, a job? If it's your heart's desires, it's never too much maybe it's just the wrong situation for you. When we don't get the thing we asked for, so many times, it feels like we just tuck our tail and take the no for an answer. But your soul is still screaming, saying but it's what I desire, why is that too much to ask for?

Over time I have learned that I don't ask too much, I just ask the wrong people. A lot of times I spent time trying to change this or exhaust myself trying to control the situation. When the truth is, I should hold my head high, realize how brave I was to ask, and then let go. I don't mean let go, like be ok with the no, I mean move on take the leap and go for what you're really asking for. Whether it be money, love, a different role, go get what you're asking for. You deserve it, you are worthy of all you're asking for. Don't let one person's "no" derail you, let it motivate you and go get what you're really asking for. Are you asking for what you really want in life?

Caged Tiger

I was chatting with the cashier at the grocery store one day when he said sometimes I start pacing back and forth here and feel like a caged tiger. We began to talk about it, how hard that would be to be taking out of where you are naturally supposed to be, live, grow and thrive. To be put in a cage in a foreign place for people to look at for the rest of your life.

Do you feel like this is how you live your life, stuck in a cage in a foreign place, pacing back and forth wanting to be free? The great news is you can be free any second you want. No one is holding you in a cage. We get the choice to follow our natural path and thrive; we get to choose to surround ourselves with what sets us free.

When you find yourself feeling caged up, remember you can choose. Get quiet and listen to the whispers of your heart, what makes you feel like you are running free, thriving in your natural environment. You have the choice to run free. Are you free or are you a caged tiger?

All The Lights On

Imagine you went through your house and turned on, the blender, hairdryer, all the TVs, all the lights and then were shocked at your power bill? Over time, I think of this scenario, and I start to laugh. Could you imagine walking into your house and everything is on? It's like a horror scene in a kid's movie.

This is what we do when we don't slow down, everything is on in the brain, overthinking, draining all our power! Take a break and turn off the overthinking brain and give yourself some peace. Sometimes all that is is taking a breath. We run around with everything on and then wonder why we are so brunt out. You don't have to solve all the world's problems, while you cook dinner and or pick up the kids. Give your self a break and turn that overthinking brain, off. Think about the good, the things that light you up, you are in charge of your thoughts, that is the most powerful thing you have.

Go through that beautiful brain of yours and one by one turn the blender off, the tv, the lights, and give yourself some peace. Imagine your sitting in the middle of a field of flowers and feel the peace. Check-in with yourself are all your lights on?

Nikki Glandon

Dance Team

Growing up, I was a dancer and a gymnast from as far back as I can remember. From middle school dance team to making the varsity team as a freshman in high school. When it came to tryouts for my senior year in high school, well, I didn't make the team. Let's just say as a 17-year old that was devastating. It crushed me for years, and I didn't even know it until later on in life. I got through that year and graduated early. But so many feelings of shame, embarrassment, and not being good enough settled in for years. How could that happen, how did I dance my whole life and all the sudden I was not good enough?

Now that I am older, with years of wisdom, and therapy, I get that it was part of my story to create growth and learn many lessons that I share with you here. I battled so long with the not good enough that cause so many other problems in life to finally realize I am the only one was saying that, I let the high school dance team thing validate it, it was my sob story or victim mentality. No one can tell you your not good enough, no job, no man, no sports team. You are in charge of that, so let it go, because you are good enough for anything you desire no matter how attached to the story you are. Just like dance team cut me, cut the things that hold you back, release them. I promise no high school dance team is worth taking away your power.

I Did Womething Wrong

So many times I don't want to make a choice because I am afraid I am going to do something wrong, that I will make the wrong choice. How many times do you stay on the fence to find what you finally decide well that opportunity is already gone. That the fear of what if it's the wrong choice stops you dead in your tracks.

Just choose already, you can't get it wrong. You will either learn from it and take the next step or continue to stay in the same place with no forward momentum. Which sounds worse making a choice so you can do the next thing or standing in quicksand. While you decide the world is still moving, it has never stopped so why would you?

We are meant to move and grow. Not worry if it's the right or wrong choice. Then when you do make a choice and it didn't work out exactly how you thought, ask yourself what could I have done differently instead of the phrase I did something wrong. So go for it, take the leap you can't get it wrong. What it one choice you can make today to move forward?

Keep The Wolves Away

I have someone in my life who is so close and dear to my heart, they almost have no idea how much they have done for me and. Don't get me wrong I have told him, how much appreciate all he has done and how much he has taught me. I mean it like sometimes it's close to impossible to really let someone know how much they have helped you. People come into our lives always at the perfect time, some stay, some continue on their own journey.

The ones that fill us up, that change our lives forever, we need to let them know, know what they mean, how special they are, even if it's scary to share how you feel. It will change their world to know they are so appreciated. This person in my life he kept the wolves away from me when I felt like I was being attacked by the world, I couldn't fight or fend for myself, I could hardly stop crying at points, but he was there by my side fighting for me when he didn't even know I needed a warrior. I didn't even know what I needed, I didn't know how deep my battle was. But God provides for us; he gave me someone to help fight for me when I couldn't.

There are times when we need warriors in our lives, someone to fight the wolves, let them help you, let them know how much you appreciate it. Sometimes we don't know what we need, but remember to trust, and you have warriors fighting for you all the time. You don't have to fight your battles alone, let those that love you fight with you.

Pirates

W e had a taxi driver in Costa Rica that said he didn't work with the taxi companies because he was a pirate. AKA he owned his own business. He was in a car with 4 women entrepreneurs, and we just embraced it, deciding we were pirates in our own business. Pirate sounds well cooler the entrepreneur and it's way easier to spell. So I have decided I am a pirate, the good kind one filled with adventure, strong and in charge of my ship.

The best part is that one of the most successful pirates in the world was a woman, Cheng I Sao she had hundreds of ships and about 50,000 in Southern China. Like most pirates she was a thief, so I am not saying embody her I am just saying stop thinking it's a man's world and you can't be powerful in it.

You can do anything you want, you can fly to the moon, build a multimillion-dollar business, you can be a housewife, a mother you can be a loving pirate commandeering your life, taking charge of your dreams. Whatever you do, do it with your superpowers, do it with poise and grace, be your own version of a pirate and sail the seas that call your name.

Parking Tickets

Why do we get mad about parking tickets? We choose not to pay the meter. The same thing is going to happen every time, don't pay the meter equals get a parking ticket. Are there times in your life where you keep doing the same thing over and over but expect different results?

Sometimes it's because you have not learned the lesson, or maybe you don't want to learn the lesson because it's not the way you like it. Like parking tickets, it's going to keep happening, any place you go, anywhere there is a meter. So why don't we learn our lesson, and approach the situation differently? Choose a higher option. In the case of the parking ticket, the higher option is to pay the meter, to follow the law that the city implemented or pay the price.

It circles back to energy again, to the universal flow of cause and effect. What you put out there you receive back. Your vibe is what is your magnetic power. So fill the universal meter with the higher option of kindness, love, and peace. Choose the higher option and you'll stop getting so many parking tickets in life.

Badass Sister

"Badass Sister" is my sister-in-law's name in my phone because nothing else suits her better, and she is a badass for so many reasons. She's from Louisiana, so she didn't grow up skiing, and I have lived in Colorado and Utah, so I have been skiing since I was 19. My family has traveled out many times for a ski vacation.

Welp one year we were having a great day and she had just crushed it coming down a black run. Next, we went to go down a blue run, only to lose her along the way. Next thing we know, my brother running up the ski hill and she was down, torn ACL and all.

It was a bummer, but I know it changed her life forever. She came back from that stronger than ever and now has completed more triathlons than I can count as well as a Half-Ironman. What I love most about this is that she was not a triathlete before, but she had to find a way to come back from her injury, and she did. She got the right trainers, the right team, and the right mindset. So often we let setbacks stop us, thinking how do I ever come back from this? You will come back from it, and you will find the inspiration to move past the challenge. Look at those around you, be inspired, and know you are just as badass they are. Always remember you've got this no matter what is in your way; do it for yourself, embrace your inner badass.

Nikki Glandon

About the Author

Nikki Glandon is excited to be introducing, *Whiskey in Your Coffee,* to the world. As a successful yoga instructor, she has helped numerous people learn how to relax, breathe and stretch their bodies and minds for over a decade. During this time, she often found her students mesmerized by her life's stories and that they wanted more stories to get them through their up and down days. *Whiskey in Your Coffee* is the result of their requests.

A life-long learner, Nikki has been intensively studying wellness & nutrition for several years and has recently added the study of Equine Assisted Learning and Equine Massage to her education repertoire. Each of these studies has shown her more and more the importance of sharing the up and down moments of life with those around us. It is her hope that *Whiskey in Your Coffee* brings each reader insights to uplift their lives and lets them know that they are never alone.

She is the founder of Brokin, and the Grit and Grace Foundation. For more information please www.brokin.com. Nikki is available for coaching or to speak at your business, organization, or civic organization. You can find out more and sign up for her newsletter at brokin.com.

Made in the USA
Coppell, TX
19 December 2019